Noah
and the
Big Boat

Noah did everything exactly as God commanded him.
—Genesis 6:22

ZONDERKIDZ

The Beginner's Bible® Noah and the Big Boat

Copyright © 2013 by Zondervan
Illustrations © 2013 by Zondervan

Requests for information should be addressed to:

Zonderkidz, 5300 Patterson Ave SE, Grand Rapids, Michigan 49530

ISBN 978-0-310-73673-8 (softcover)

Editor: Mary Hassinger
Cover & interior design: Cindy Davis

Printed in China

14 15 16 17 18 19 /LPC/ 12 11 10 9 8 7 6 5 4 3 2

ZONDERVAN.com/
AUTHORTRACKER
follow your favorite authors

When God made the world, everything was perfect. The grass was green. The sky was blue. The trees and flowers were pretty. And the birds sang happy songs.

God made a man and a woman to live in this perfect world. But soon the man and woman disobeyed God's one rule. God still loved them, but his world was not perfect anymore.

After a while, many more people lived in the world. They did not always love God or obey him. They were mean to each other and did some very bad things.

God was sad that the people were so bad. He was sorry that he had made people to live in his beautiful world.

But there was one man who loved God. His name was Noah. Noah's family loved God too. God was happy that Noah and his family loved him.

One day, God said to Noah, "The people do not obey me. They do bad things every day. I do not want them to live in my world anymore. I am going to send a flood to wash everything away." But God wanted Noah to be safe. So God told Noah to build a big boat.

"You must build an ark from wood," God said. "It needs to be very big and tall. Make rooms in the ark and cover it with tar. It will be for you and your family. It will also be for the animals. Two of every kind will come to you."

Noah did not know how to build an ark. But God told him just what to do. Noah listened to God and did everything God told him to do.

Noah worked very hard every day. It took many years for Noah to build the ark. But Noah never gave up. He worked, and he worked, and he worked.

Finally the ark was finished. Now it was time to put the animals inside. The animals came to Noah two-by-two, just like God said they would.

Noah led the animals into the ark. Birds and bears. Rabbits and dogs. Turtles and donkeys. Cats and spiders. Every kind of animal went into the ark.

Noah had to bring a lot of food into the ark for his family and for all the animals.

Some of the animals were much harder to get into the ark! But Noah obeyed God and did everything God told him to do.

Noah finally got all the food and animals into the ark. Then it was time for Noah and his family to go into the ark too. When everyone was safe inside, God closed the door.

Big raindrops began to fall from the sky. It rained and rained and rained. It rained for forty days and forty nights. Soon the whole earth was covered with water. Even the tallest mountains were covered with water.

Noah and his family were safe and dry inside the ark. The animals were safe too. And they all had enough food to eat. God kept them safe, just like he had promised.

The rain finally stopped. But Noah and his family and all the animals had to stay inside the ark for many more days.

God sent a wind to blow across the water to make the flood go away. Noah opened a window in the ark and sent out a dove. He was hoping the dove could find some dry land. But soon the dove came back to the ark. The water was still too high.

One week later, Noah sent the dove out again. This time the dove came back with a leaf in its mouth. Noah knew that the flood was almost gone. He sent the dove out one more time. This time the dove did not come back. Noah knew they would soon be able to come out of the ark.

Bump! "What was that?" asked Noah. He looked over the side of the ark. Noah saw that the water was drying up. "It's time for you and your family to leave the ark," God told Noah. "Let all the animals out too!"

Noah and his family and all the animals came out of the ark. Noah thanked God for keeping them safe. God said to Noah, "I promise I will never send another flood to cover the earth." Then God put a beautiful rainbow in the sky.